LET'S THINK
ABOUT NATURE!

LET'S THINK ABOUT NATURE!

KAROLYN FRANCOISE VERVILLE, PH.D

To order additional copies of this book, contact:
Xlibris Corporation
1-888-795-4274
www.Xlibris.com
Orders@Xlibris.com
110876

CONTENTS

PREFACE

This program is designed to complement the natural sciences. Scientific concepts, while usually can be defined by specific criteria and procedures for classification, tend to look for inert information instead of dynamic information.

This dynamism is what we promote here. That blood is "red" or that water is "colorless" are given knowledge that hardly encourages questioning or reflection. But let's suppose that it provides more information about the actual conditions of observation: it is said that the blood is red "under the naked eye" or that water is colorless "in small quantity". Suppose also that in this case students are aware that what is true in parts need not be true for the whole, and vice versa.

These students can be motivated to reflect and ask if blood continues to be red under a microscope or if water is without color in large quantities.

In other words, to lead reflection with practice is what enhances the thinking abilities that should be inculcated in *Let's Think about nature* and these thinking skills cannot be achieved without a certain philosophical curiosity.

There are several thinking abilities generated by philosophical questioning and transmitted to other disciplines through reading, writing, oral expression and the ability to pay attention.

Here's some of them: providing reasons; asking questions; reasoning with matrices; inductive and deductive reasoning; causal thinking; standardization; immediate inferences; hypothetical reasoning; making inference; formation of concepts; discovery of assumptions; classification; description; realization of distinctions. instantiation; finding similarities; recognizing the relationship between part and whole and mean-end; argumentation; discriminative meanings; making comparisons; acknowledging ambiguities; defining; telling stories, etc.

It would be quite exhausting to enumerate all the thinking skills and mental abilities promoted by philosophical questioning in the natural sciences, but these few are sufficient to give a general idea of how *Let's Think About Nature* can promote the development of children.

INTRODUCTION TO EDUCATORS

Reasoning about nature . . . what could it be? There is a considerable overlap between ecology and environmental ethics, since the cognitive abilities we promote through exercises also are useful for the formation of concepts, and the conceptual clarification obtained following discussion plans can also be invaluable to provide a structure of understanding, in whose terms cognitive skills training can make some sense for children and teachers alike.

While a program of environmental ethics touches the topics of the two sciences, zoology and ecology, it is designed to be a complement to these sciences rather than a substitute for them. Sciences are incomparable in their experience to instill in students an understanding of the nature through observation and experimentation. Unfortunately, the pedagogy of science educators have used in order to motivate the students to observe and experiment has left much to be desired.

Many educators of science have taken as axiomatic the fact that children are abysmally ignorant of the nature, but at the same time, fortunately, are incredibly curious and inquisitive. These educators have come to the conclusion that it seems natural that children are overly grateful when they are shown the truths about nature, which science teachers are eager to offer.

On the one hand, the curiosity with which the majority of children start kindergarten should be strengthened in a consistent and persistent manner if you want to keep curiosity alive, and the facts seem to indicate that by the fourth-grade more or less, the natural curiosity that many children had exhibited previously, for this stage, has declined greatly.

On the other hand, at this age, children have built an extensive network of hypotheses and theories and they explain themselves how the world works. Scientists can observe these as primitive myths and take for granted that children immediately accept the opportunity to exchange their myths with the truths offered by science.

If we wish to forgo their points of view on nature, we must be prepared to discuss honestly with them the reasons why they should do it, and we have to discuss with equal candor their reasons when they think that we need to take their points of view. Without these open discussions, we will not only fail to not to show them the world as it is, which is indeed a matter of little importance, but the most important aspect is that we will fail in the attempt to make them think scientifically and enthusiastically participate in the questioning. But these discussions must be kept reasonable, as logically disciplined discussions. We not only nurture their own concepts, we have to reason with them. What about the rest? It will be a matter for you to discover!

HOW TO USE THIS MANUAL

Against the perennial doctrine of education, **Let's Think About Nature** has the intention of promoting mental acts, such as recalling; assuming; imagining; conceiving; distinguishing; anticipating; caring thinking; deliberating; considering; affirming; abstracting; noting; observing; studying; generalizing; learning; memorizing; listing; planning; proposing; predicting; concluding, and so on.

Children must first sit in a circle, so that they can see each other, and read the text in question, until the next sign of punctuation or something like that. Then educator, at random, will choose questions from the plan for discussion and propose them to the class.

Students will be more than eager to try and find what may be the answer, and give their reasons for this. There may not be an answer to certain questions, or children could be metaphysically answering any of them. In this case, often the experiments will help to answer these paradoxes. Children should openly discuss their views among themselves, within the dynamics of the group. It is important to identify here that it has been shown that democracy in the classroom helps in developing reasoning skills through self-esteem. If the children's answers are quite focused, congratulate them. If they are completely missing the point, thank them anyway for sharing their point of views.

As you will observed, the questions provided in the discussion plans and in the text itself could have no relation to one another. **Let's Think About Nature** is about finding how and why things are the way they are, and not otherwise.

Children think constantly, and reflect on what they think. The promise of philosophical inquiry is to help us think better and also to better reflect upon things. Students also acquire knowledge constantly, and then try to use what they know in their everyday life. The task here is to help them in applying their knowledge in the most effective way, making better judgments in the course of their lives. Immerse yourself with them in the philosophical journey of natural sciences and don't be surprised if the results astonish you!

WARNING

All of the experiments suggested in this manual shall be carried out in the presence of an adult. Children should use old clothes or overalls.

If they are working on a table, they must protect it with paper or cardboard.

If they are using fire, they must light matches away from their bodies. Matches must be left to cool off before throwing them away. When working with hot objects, they must use insulating gloves.

They should not be walking around or play or run when handling scissors. Scissors have must have rounded edges.

Children should not play with electrical wires because they can lead to death.

If they are managing small animals, explain to students that living beings also feel pain; they are not toys and should be handled with great care and respect.

After the experiments, children must return things to where they belong and wash their hands.

THE ELEMENTS

What is the world made of? In ancient times, people thought that the four elements: water, air, fire and earth were what the world was made of. They said that this was the basic raw material and therefore thought that matter was made of elements. The elements can be found in different states: solid (earth, ice), gas (fire, air) or liquid (water). But the water can be found in the three states. Due to these states, we can say that nothing in nature is created and nothing is lost, everything is transformed from one state to another.

The Greek philosophers

Thales of Miletus

Thales of Miletus (624-548 B.C.E) thought that the first of the four elements was **water** because we find it everywhere. With this began the first natural sciences.

Anaximander of Miletus (585-525 B.C.E) considered that the **air** was the source of all life. Due to the fact that the air expands or condenses, it causes fire, water and earth. Particular realities come from the density of the air.

Anaxagoras (500-428 B.C.E) thought that the **fire** was the first element because without heat, nothing could exist.

PLAN OF DISCUSSION ON THE ELEMENTS

1- Where do the elements come from?

2- What would happen if there were no elements?

3- What do you think would be the first element of all and why?

4- A diamond is very hard. Is it possible that a diamond be turned into gas?

5- A rock is very hard. Do you think it could ever turn into a liquid?

6- Why science began with studying the elements?

7- What are the properties of the elements?

8- Are your feelings made of elements?

9- Is your thinking made of elements?

10- Are your dreams made of elements?

11- Are you made of elements?

12- Do you think you could turn into a gas?

WATER

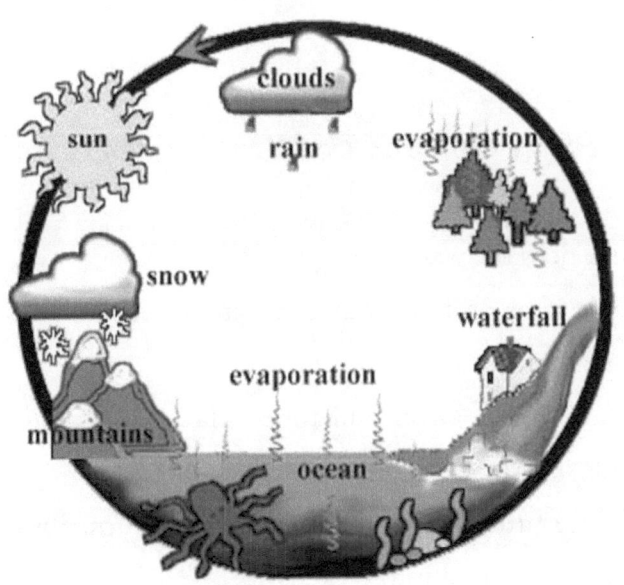

Water is a liquid. It is colorless, odorless and tasteless (unflavored) in small quantity. Scientists refer to it as H20 because it is composed of two gases: one molecule of hydrogen and two molecules of oxygen. Water can also be solid (ice) or gas (steam). Pure water freezes at 0 (zero) degrees Celsius and boils at 100 (one hundred) degrees Celsius. The weight of your body is composed of 60% to 70% of water. Hydrogen is the molecule most encountered in the universe; it is present in space and also found on our planet.

Water covers approximately 75% of the Earth's surface. Water erodes the Earth, transports it away and returns to settle elsewhere. Water is necessary for life and at the same time, it must be pure so that it is suitable for consumption. This means that populations and cities often must have facilities for the purification of water. In some parts of the world, the power of water is a large source of energy. Without the presence of water, the geography is changed into deserts.

PLAN OF DISCUSSION ON WATER

1- Where does the water come from?

2- Is there water around us that we cannot see?

3- What are the properties of the water?

4- What makes the water sometimes solid, gaseous and other times liquid?

5- If the ice turns into water and the water turns into steam, the steam is converted into what?

6- When you cry your tears are liquid? Could your tears ever become ice or a gas?

7- What is the pollution of water? What happens when water is contaminated?

8- What class of substances you think can be found in the water?

9- How can we produce very pure water?

10- How are the ocean water and the water we drink different?

11- Why water in large quantities is always represented as blue color?

12- What makes water be without color in small amounts?

EXPERIMENTATION WITH WATER

Water pressure

Material: -an empty plastic bottle

-a nail

-water

Fill the bottle with water. With the nail, drill 3 holes one above the other half way into the bottle.

As you can see the water comes out with more pressure in the hole below that in the holes above. This is because the water pressure is higher in more depth. This pressure of the water is used on turbines to create energy among the industries and the factories. Even certain houses benefit from the energy created by the water.

Strength of turbines

Material: -a cork

-a nail

-scissors

-a clean plastic (such as yogurt) container

-water

Punch the nail through the cork and cut the container of yoghurt into small rectangles. Insert the rectangles in the cork. Now put your turbine under a stream of water and observe it spin!

The water pressure has been used for centuries to generate energy within the industries. These turbines are called hydraulic. We also use these turbines to spin generators, which produces electricity. Approximately 3% of all electricity produced in the world comes from the pressure of the water and is an inexhaustible source. The word "hydro" in Greek means: water.

The electricity created by the water pressure in the turbines is called: hydroelectricity.

AIR

The air is a mixture of various gases. The main gases that make up air are nitrogen (78%) and oxygen (21%). Other substances found in the air are water vapor and impurities. The air is odorless, colorless and tasteless in small quantities, and blue in larger quantities.

You can feel the air when it's windy outside. We can observe the air when we make soap bubbles. We can listen to the air when we blow in a flute. We can smell the air when it has many impurities.

We have to breathe the air to keep on living. Indeed, all living beings on earth need oxygen to live, without which they would die. When we inhale air, we exhale gas called carbon dioxide and water vapor. This carbon dioxide is what plants and trees breathe, and they exhale oxygen that we breathe in again. If we cut all trees, they could no longer produce oxygen for the rest of the planet. The largest rain forest in the world is the tropical forest of the Amazons in Latin America. It is truly the lungs of the planet.

Hot air is lighter than cold air and that is why hot air tends to rise up while the cold air stays closer to the ground. Birds can fly in the air, aided by the warm air. These hot air flows are called "thermal". The winds are created by mixing high and low pressure of cold air and warm air.

PLAN OF DISCUSSION ON AIR

1- Where does the air come from?

2- Where can we find the air?

3- What does it mean to be transported by air?

4- What could travel through the air?

5- What is air pollution?

6- Are the atmosphere and air the same thing?

7- Is there air in the space?

8- Why is hot air lighter than cold air?

9- What would happen if the trees or plants didn't exist?

10- What would happen if there were no air?

11- Can air sometimes be solid or liquid?

12- How can we produce very clean air?

EXPERIMENTATION WITH AIR

The force of air

Material: -a nail
-hard cardboard
-a plastic tube
-adhesive tape
-a piece of wood

Cut an arrow onto the cardboard. Fix the plastic tube on it with adhesive tape. Insert the nail into the piece of wood and then inserted the arrow and the tube of plastic on the nail. Watch how it turns when you blow.

The energy created by the wind is called "Aeolian". The windmills are based on this principle and have been used for grinding grains in Asia since 2,400 years ago. The wings of the windmill must be against the wind to make them effective. The word "eo" in Greek means: air.

Observing the air

Material: -a large glass bowl
-a empty glass
-water

Fill the bowl with water. Turn the glass down and place it in the bowl of water. Tilt the glass. Can you observe the air bubbles that come out?

Hot air and cold air

Material: -Two balloons

-A source of heat (such as a radiator)

-A source of cold (such as refrigerator)

Inflate the two balloons so that they have roughly the same size. Place one of them on the radiator. The balloon will get bigger due to heat. Place the other balloon in the refrigerator. This one will decrease in size due to the cold. Compare the difference in size of the two balloons. The heat causes the air to expand, and thus lightens it. The cold causes the air to contract and therefore makes it heavier.

THE FIRE

The fire is a reaction created by the burning of a substance, and results in light, heat and flame. Without the oxygen that we find in the air, the fire cannot exist. The flames can be obtained through an extreme source of heat, such as friction. We believe that the fire was discovered by rubbing two pieces of wood together or banging two rocks (called "flints") to get a spark.

The sun is a ball of fire that burns gas in space. The sun is located thousands and thousands of miles away from us, and yet we can feel its heat on hot days. All living creatures need the effects of the sun in order to live. The sun is what we call "daylight". Without light, we cannot see the colors. All colors are included in the light. Light is a wave (and sometimes a particle). The colors are the result of the vibration of this wave.

The rainbows in the sky are formed by bands of colors. These bands are made by the so-called primary colors: red, orange, yellow, green, blue, Indigo and violet. These bands of colors are called the "spectrum". The same spectrum can be seen in a rainbow when light passes through the rain or drops of water, which acts as a prism.

With the higher vibration of the light wave, the color we will find will be at the red end of the spectrum. While with the lowest vibration of the light wave, the color obtained will be at the violet end of the spectrum. These are called "infrared" and "ultraviolet".

We can see the colors due to the reflection of light. For example, your shirt is blue because when light shines on it, your shirt absorbs all colors contained in the light except blue, which is the one reflected. This gives as a result, a blue shirt.

PLAN OF DISCUSSION ON FIRE

1- Where does the sun come from?

2- If there is no oxygen in space, how can the sun be burning?

3- Where does the sun go after the sunset?

4- Where does the sun come from when it comes out in the morning?

5- Are stars suns?

6- Where do the colors go when there is no light?

7- Are there colors that we cannot see?

8- What are the dangers of fire? How can we prevent them?

9- Can fire be liquid or solid?

10- What are the properties of the fire?

11- What is the relationship between fire and electricity?

12- Is light a type of electricity?

EXPERIMENTATION WITH FIRE

Color Spectrum

Material: -a light source (a flashlight or an electric lamp)

-Two prisms

Shine the light into the prism. From the prism emerges a set of bands of bright colors. Now take the second prism and place it in a way that the spectrum of the other prism falls on it. Can you see how they combine all colors into a white light?

Need of oxygen

Material: -a candle

-an empty glass

-water

-a deep bowl

Light the candle. Place the empty glass over it. Can you see how the flame extinguishes? Now pour some water into the bowl. Place the candle inside. Lit the candle again and place the empty glass over the candle. As the flame goes off, the water level in the glass rises to fill the place of oxygen that the candle has burned.

THE EARTH

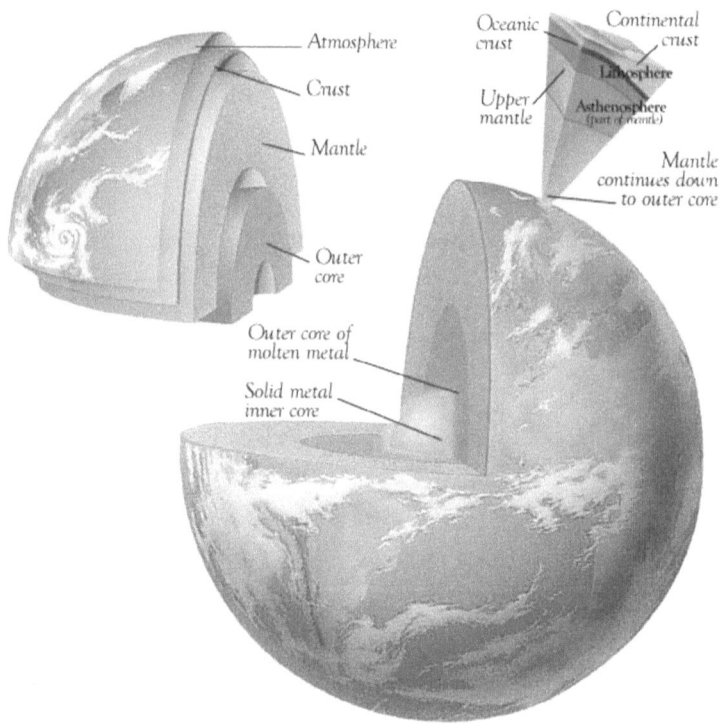

The Earth is the planet on which we live. It is the third planet of our solar system, located between Mars and Venus. The earth rotates on its axis, and spins around the sun. A complete loop over itself creates the days and nights. A complete revolution around the Sun determines the length of a year.

The Earth is an inorganic matter (not alive); it crumbles easily, and is composed of soil. The soil is the solid part of the planet, often opposed to the water and air. The soil is the raw material on which grows the vegetation and living organisms. Another name which refers to the Earth is "Pan Gaia", meaning "Mother Earth", because all living things are born on it. We cultivate the soil in order to obtain fruits and vegetable to eat. The Earth is also known as the "Blue Planet", since it is covered by 75% of water.

The people in the antiquity like **Ptolemy** (100-170 B.C.E) thought that the Earth was flat, immobile, in the center of the universe, and everything revolved around it. This point of view of the universe is known as "Ptolemaic" (or egocentric).

Many, many years later, **Copernicus** (1473-1543) A.C.E suggested that Earth had movement; that the Sun is in the center of our solar system, and everything revolves around it. He also suggested that the Earth is round and slightly flattened at the poles. Therefore, we live in a "Copernican" (or geocentric) point of view. The Greek word "geo" means: "Earth". The word "ego" in Latin means: "self"

Gravity is a physical property of the Earth. We can only see its effect, as when a loose object falls to the floor. Things fall because they are attracted to the ground by a force. This force is the: "universal gravitational force". It was **Isaac Newton** (1687 A.C.E.) who discovered gravity, while taking a nap under an apple tree. An apple suddenly fell on his head and he thus understood that all objects are attracted like a magnet to the ground.

PLAN OF DISCUSSION ON THE EARTH

1- Where does the Earth come from?

2- What is the Earth made of?

3- Can the soil be liquid or gaseous?

4- Is it correct to think about the Earth as a mother?

5- Is Earth the only habitable planet in the solar system?

6- Is Earth the only habitable planet in the universe?

7- Why did people of antiquity believed that the Earth was flat?

8- Why did people of antiquity believed that the Sun revolved around the Earth?

9- Is really the sun in the center of the solar system?

10- Where does gravity come from?

11- Could there be a giant magnet inside the Earth?

12- What would happen if there were no gravity?

EXPERIMENTATION WITH THE EARTH

Growing a seed

Material: -an empty cup (like a Styrofoam cup)

-fresh dirt

-seeds (flowers or vegetables)

-water

-Sunlight (or a lamp with a light bulb for plants)

Pour dirt into the cup. With your finger, make a hole in the dirt of about 5 cm. Gently deposit the seeds in the hole and cover them with soil. Pour a little water and placed the cup in an area illuminated by the Sun. Keep the soil moist, and be sure to not let it dry completely. Wait approximately two weeks and watch the plant grow!

Law of Attraction

Material: -magnets

-needles or pins, or several small metal objects.

To demonstrate the universal gravitational force, you can use two magnets to see the attraction of things. Place the magnets on a table. Place the needles near them. Can you see how the needles are attracted to the magnets? The needles are attracted to the magnets in the same way that objects are attracted to the ground.

THE PROCESS OF LIFE

What is the process of life and where does it come from? How things can be alive? It seems that the combinations of plants and animals that may have descendants are part of the process of life. If it is born, then it will die. What can this mean?

The first book of botany and biological classification of animals was written by **Aristotle** in a book called "*De Animalus Partibus*" (meaning: on the parts of animals) in 312 B.C.E. Botany and biology have always fascinated the great thinkers. What is life and why are we alive? Where does the life go when living things die? These questions are exactly what triggered the natural sciences: in order to understand life, humans have created official classifications of animals and plants.

ABOUT PLANTS

Plants are living beings without mouth, without nervous system or organs of locomotion. They are characterized by leaves, roots and stems (or trunks in the case of trees). They have no blood, but instead they have what we call "sap" or "resin". Plants are usually green due to their chlorophyll.

The flowers, vegetables, fruits, trees, fungi and some bacteria are plant. Generally speaking, all green plants inhale carbon dioxide, and exhale the oxygen we need to be able to be alive. The flowers are different because they inhale oxygen and exhale carbon dioxide, like us. The scientific study of plants is called "Botany".

All the plants transform light into chlorophyll. This is called "photosynthesis". We use chlorophyll to produce certain chewing gum that is green. Remember the small seed in the Styrofoam cup? The plant grows upwards and roots grow down. No one really knows why or how, but it is the case. Plants need dirt, water, air and light to live. But like other living beings, they also die. Many fabrics used in the manufacture of clothing are made from plants, such as cotton and flax. Cereals are wheat, oats, soybeans and bran. With wheat and corn, we obtain the flour used in many recipes for cooking.

The trees are plants that usually have a single trunk, and have branches at some distance from the ground. Some trees have more than one trunk and some shrubs have only a resemblance to a trunk or a stem. However, the trees generally are higher than the bushes and have larger trunk than shrubs stems.

Some trees drop their leaves regularly at the end of the growing season: these trees are known as trees "deciduous". Other trees drop their leaves gradually, over a period of years. These trees are called "coniferous" and "Evergreen broad-leaved". Coniferous trees produce resin, a very thick and sticky substance, which is not soluble in water but is soluble in alcohol. We use this resin as a fuel.

There are two kind of sap: the ascendant sap comes from the roots and rises up to the leaves and the descending sap which is produced from the leaves down to the roots. Maple syrup is made with the ascending sap of the maple tree.

PLAN OF DISCUSSION ON PLANTS

1- Where do plants come from?

2- What are plants made of?

3- Why are there plants?

4- Think about vegetables?

5- Do plants feel pain, for example, if we cut a tree or a flower?

6- Can plants bleed?

7- Do plants have rights?

8- Can you think about other products made of plants?

9- What would happen if there were no plants?

10- How are marine plants and other plants different?

11- How are wildflowers and cultivated flowers different?

12- What does it mean when a person is in a "vegetative" state?

EXPERIMENTATION WITH PLANTS

Observing sap

Material: -3 branches of celery

-3 empty jars

-food colorant (blue and red)

-water

-sunlight

Empty the same amount of water in the three jars. Add the food colorant in two of these jars, leaving the third on with clear water. Place the branches of celery in these jars and put the jars in a place with sun light. Wait a few days. Can you observe how the branches of celery in the colored water are no longer green and took the color of the water in the jars?

Water and light are the basic of all plant nutrients, because they feed on chlorophyll. When the water is clear, then the plant is green, but by adding color to the water it also give color to the plant, affecting the color of chlorophyll.

ABOUT ANIMALS

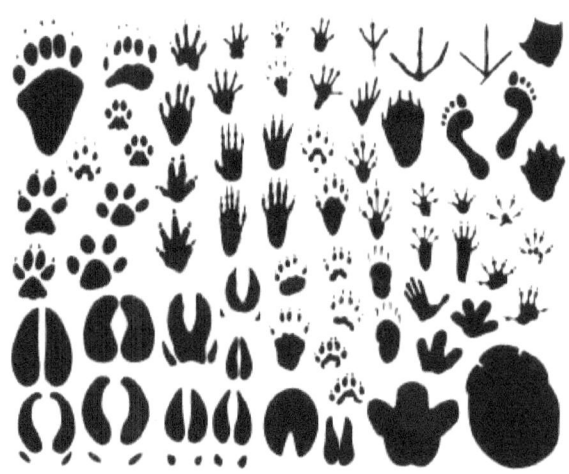

Animals are living beings, endowed with movements and sensitivity. They are able to search for food and eating solid food. In certain parts of the world, animals have rights that protect them from being killed and eaten by humans. Some species are endangered species: these species also have rights to not be hunted, such as whales, pandas, some wolves, tortoises, elephants, lions, koalas, etc.

René Descartes (A.C.E 1649) was a French philosopher that regarded animals as machines: he thought that animals didn't think and were programmed to look for their food. Also, he believed that animals didn't feel pain.

Lamarck and **Darwin** (1890 A.C.E.) said that animals came from other animals, for example, that men came from the monkeys, that birds came from reptiles, etc. They also believed that nothing was created, everything evolved. This was called "the theory of evolution". Currently, we know that this theory in its entirety is no longer relevant, but we accept that there is some parallelism (similarities) between species, for example apes resemble humans, both birds and most reptiles lay eggs, or wolves resemble dogs, and so forth.

The theory of evolution is opposed to the "creationist theory" which says that everything was created, and that certain things have evolved (such as human technology, for example).

Human beings are considered animals because they seek their own food, breathe oxygen, sleep, reproduce and they are equipped with movement. There are few differences between humans and other animals: we walk on two feet (bipeds), our thumb is opposed to the rest of the fingers which gives us more agility. Also we have an organized and complex system of language, and we can laugh, cry, and reason.

In order to understand the world around us, human beings created different classifications of what we found was similar and different from animals. Therefore we have categories such as: invertebrate and vertebrate animals, types of vegetarian animals (preys) and carnivores (predators) etc.

Some animals eat only plants, such as rodents (mice, rats, rabbits, etc.) and cattle (cows, goats) for example, and these animals are called "vegetarian" because they eat only plants. Other animals eat only meat, such as felines (the cat family: panthers, lions, tigers, cats, etc.) or the canines (the dog family: wolves, foxes, dogs, etc.) for example, and these are called "carnivorous".

In the natural food chain, the plant is food to the vegetarian, which in turn is food to the carnivore. Carnivores usually don't eat other carnivores, unless necessary to survive.

The predators are characterized by their dentition: four canines made for tearing meat, while the preys have square posterior teeth for chewing plants.

Some other animals are both vegetarians and carnivores: they are called "omnivorous", such as humans and bears, for example. Other animals are called "insectivores" because they eat insects, such as birds, fish, reptiles, and some mammals.

PLAN OF DISCUSSION ON ANIMALS

1- Where do animals come from?

2- Do animals really have rights?

3- Can you think about other species of animals that are in danger of extinction?

4- Is it bad if a species of animal disappears?

5- Do you believe in the evolution of things or the creation of things?

6- What creates what and what evolves from what?

7- Do you think, as Descartes, that the animals are like machines and do not feel pain?

8- Why can we laugh, cry, reasoning, and speak a language?

9- How is it that we can walk on two feet?

10- Why do we classify things in order to understand them?

11- Are humans preys or predators?

12- Do we have total power over animals?

ABOUT THE INVERTEBRATES

Invertebrate animals are a group of animals without backbones; like crustaceans (lobsters, crabs), insects, arachnids (spiders), worms, mollusks, sea urchins, etc.

Just because they have no back bones doesn't mean they do not have a spinal cord. The spinal cord is responsible for the nervous system. It is located in the spinal canal, and transmits the nerve flow between the brain and organs, all the way towards the extremities.

Therefore, instead of having bones in the back that support all the body, these animals have an equivalent, such as a shell or an exoskeleton that protects their spinal cord and their organs.

ABOUT THE VERTEBRATES

Vertebrates are animals that are characterized by having a spinal cord protected by the spine. These animals are divided into five classes: oviparous (birds), reptiles, amphibians, fish and mammals.

The spine in humans consists of 33 vertebrae: 7 cervical, 12 dorsal, 5 lumbar, 5 sacred and 4 coccyges. The spinal cord is located within the spinal column. Within the spinal cord, there is a liquid called the "rachitic liquid", which is responsible for all the nervous system. The function of the spinal column is to protect the rachitic liquid in the spinal cord, because if this suffers damage, it can cause paralysis (lost partial or full sensation, motor, and reflexes) of the lower limbs (legs) and/or the upper limbs (arms), depending on the affected site of spinal cord, and how much liquid has been lost.

PLAN OF DISCUSSION ON INVERTEBRATES AND VERTEBRATES

1- Why do some animals have vertebrae and others do not?
2- Are humans animals?
3- In what are humans similar to animals and in what are we different from animals?
4- What are the advantages of having bones in the back?
5- What are the advantages of being an invertebrate?
6- Can you feel your bones in your back?
7- What is paralysis?
8- Do you know someone with paralysis?
9- How do people with paralysis live?
10- How can injury to the back be prevented?

EXPERIMENTATION ON THE SPINAL CORD

What does it mean to be paralyzed?

Material: -chairs

Ask some of the students to sit on the chairs. Tell them they are not allowed to stand up. Ask other children to put their hands in their pants' pockets. Tell them they cannot take their hands off their pockets. Ask students to go on and do their normal activities. After 10 minutes, ask them how they feel about being unable to run, walk, draw or write, so they will have a general idea of what it might means to be paralyzed.

Another good exercise would be visiting patients at the local Centre of paralysis. Appointments can be arranged with the director of the Department. These trips can be a revelation for the awareness of students on the dangers to their health and their bodies, as well as to develop emphatic social behaviors.

ABOUT THE OVIPAROUS

The oviparous are a class of animals that lay eggs, like birds, fish, amphibians and reptiles. There is only one mammal that lays eggs and it is called the "Platypus". The egg is known as the oldest symbol of life in the world.

The birds are oviparous vertebrates, covered with feathers, have wings to fly, a beak and warm red blood. They cover their eggs in a nest until they hatch. There are more than 10, 000 species of birds known in today's world.

The Platypus is a mammal; with a beak like a duck, and this animal lays eggs but nurse their babies. How different is this animal! It stands out in almost all the classifications of animals except that of reptiles/ amphibians (because it is a mammal).

While the birds usually fly, the ostrich and the emu and the rhea are too big to fly, so they have small wings that are not functional. However they can run very fast, up to 40 km/h! Their eggs are very large: they have a diameter of 30 cm.

The eggs of chickens are made of a viscous white substance rich in albumin, a yellow yolk, and a small air chamber. This smooth part of the egg is protected by the eggshell. These eggs are brooded by the body heat of the chicken, until the time for hatching has arrived (21 days) and then the hens slowly break the eggshell. The babies use the small chamber of air to breathe, because to be born is very hard work.

Even though the eggs of chickens are very different from the eggs of fish or reptiles, they share the same principle. The "embryo" (unformed baby) grows inside the egg until it is ready to hatch from it. We eat eggs from chicken and fish, when they are not "fertilized" (without the embryo). The eggs of the fish are called "caviar" and are very nutritious.

The fish and the reptiles do not sit on their eggs like birds do, because their bodies do not have heat. These animals are cold-blooded. Instead, they lay their eggs in the water (in the case of fish and amphibians) or in the sand (in the case of reptiles) and it is the heat of the sun which leads the eggs to hatching time. In the case of turtles, crocodiles and alligators, the temperature of the sand is what determines if the babies will be females or males.

PLAN OF DISCUSSION ON THE OVIPAROUS

1- Where do eggs come from?

2- Where do oviparous come from?

3- What came first, the egg or the oviparous?

4- What came first, the chicken or the egg?

5- Do insects lay eggs?

6- Is it possible that humans also come from eggs?

7- Is it possible that all living beings come from eggs?

8- Why is the egg a symbol of life?

9- Are all eggs edible?

10- Are the eggs we eat fertilized?

EXPERIMENTATION ON THE OVIPAROUS

Hatching eggs

Material: -fertilized eggs (available at a local farm)

-source of constant heat (like the restaurants hot lamp)

-Empty fish tank

-Straw

Place the straw on the bottom of the tank. Place the fertilized eggs in the tank and set the lamp at the top of the tank to provide an uninterrupted and continuous source of heat. Two times a day, you must turn the eggs. It is good idea to mark with an "X" one side of the egg, and a "0" the other side of the egg, to know when it was rotated. Wait 21 days and observe the miracle of life! Once born, the chicks can be returned to the local farm where you took the eggs.

A good exercise would be to have students write a diary in which they draw the embryo and describe the activity inside the egg on a daily basis, in order to observe the progress made.

ABOUT REPTILES

Reptiles are the oldest animals known on Earth. They are oviparous vertebrates have scales on their bodies. They are cold-blooded and need the heat of the sun to warm up. They are classified into four major divisions: lizards, snakes, turtles and crocodiles. Some of them are vegetarians, and some others are carnivorous or insectivorous. Most reptiles lay their eggs in the sand, and it is the heat of the sun that makes the eggs hatch. It is also the same heat from the sun that determines if the babies will be females or males.

The dinosaurs were also reptiles. They were the largest reptiles (up to 30 meters), but have now disappeared from the surface of the planet. Many dinosaur fossils have been found in various parts of the world. Some of them were vegetarians, and some other carnivores. About the dinosaurs, there are two theories that are opposed one to another: one that says that their blood was cold, another that says they were warm-blooded.

ABOUT AMPHIBIANS

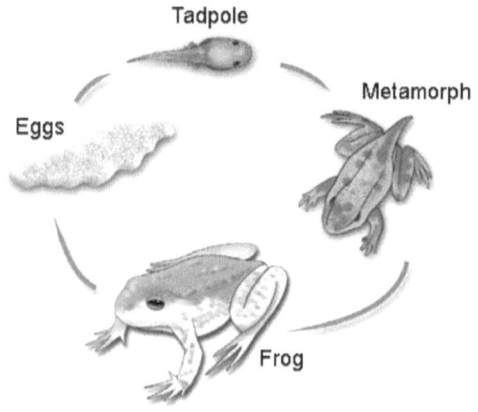

Amphibians are a class of animals that need to be in the water and out of water to live. They live in ponds, lakes and rivers and need to move to the land to rest and to warm up. This is the case of the frog and the crocodile. Amphibians breathe the air with their lungs, but also breathe through their skin, which is composed of millions of small holes. Amphibians are a subclass of reptiles.

The frog lays its eggs in the water. When comes the time for the egg to hatch, the baby frog looks like a small fish and is called a "tadpole". Little by little, they grow legs and the tadpole loses his tail to become a fully developed frog. When it is the winter season, the frog is hiding under the ground and sleeps during all the season. This behavior is known as "state of hibernation".

PLAN OF DISCUSSION ON REPTILES AND AMPHIBIANS

1- Where do reptiles come from?

2- Why are there reptiles?

3- What is the difference between reptiles and amphibians?

4- Why are the reptiles the oldest animals on Earth?

5- Are all reptiles oviparous?

6- Why did the dinosaurs disappear?

7- Would dinosaurs have disappeared if they hibernated?

8- Do you know any other animal that hibernates?

9- Do reptiles have rights?

10- Are all reptiles dangerous?

EXPERIMENTATION ON AMPHIBIANS

The frog in hibernation

Material: -a frog

-an empty tank

-1 kg of ice

-2 kg of fresh dirt

Pour the dirt in the tank. Place the frog in the tank. Place the ice on the ground leaving a 15 cm by 15 cm square without ice for the frog. Look at the behavior of the frog, the way in which it buries itself into the ground and falls asleep after an hour, approximately. Many other animals Hibernate when it is cold outside, such as the squirrel and the bear for example. This behavior is more common in the countries of the North where the temperature drops a lot. It is a way to survive without having to eat regularly, which saves the life of many animals because the reserves of food diminish during the cold seasons.

ABOUT MAMMALS

Mammals are a class of animals which are characterized by breastfeeding their baby with the mother's milk. Generally speaking, they have hair, two lungs and a heart with 4 cavities. They are warm-blooded. They are vertebrates, but do not lay eggs, except for the famous platypus.

There are more than 5,000 species of mammals. Humans are mammals also. We can separate mammals into two categories: inferior mammals (rodents and cats) and superior mammals (humans and great apes). Superior mammals are distinguished from inferior mammals because they can learn complex behavior, such as communication. They can also use tools to facilitate their existence. In the classification of mammals, we can find both predators and prey.

PLAN OF DISCUSSION ON MAMMALS

1- Where do mammals come from?

2- Why are there mammals?

3- How are human mammals?

4- Do all mammals breastfeed their babies?

5- How can males be mammal if they do not breastfeed their babies?

6- What is the difference between inferior and superior mammals?

7- Why are some pets mammals and others not?

8- Do mammals have rights?

9- Do humans have a responsibility towards mammals?

10- Do you have responsibilities towards your pets?

EXPERIMENTATION ON MAMMALS

The agility of the mouse

Material: -a white mouse

-a thin string of 2 meters long

Ask two students to hold each end of the string. The string must be 1 meter from the floor. Place the mouse on the string. The mouse will travel from one end of the string to the other using its tail as a corkscrew in order to keep its balance. This shows perfectly the agility of lower mammals.

A good idea would be to have a pet in the classroom, such as a hamster or a Guinea pig. Students may have responsibilities with the class pet: one feeds it, another cleans the box, another gives it water, and so on. We are responsible for the animals that we decide to take care of and it would be a good opportunity to familiarize students with the care of animals.

* NO ANIMAL WAS HURT DURING THE EXPERIMENTS SUGGESTED IN THIS MANUAL.

www.ingramcontent.com/pod-product-compliance
Lightning Source LLC
Chambersburg PA
CBHW061226280526
45784CB00006B/2656